THE NEXT MONSTERS

also by Julie Doxsee

Undersleep (2008)
Objects for a Fog Death (2010)

The Next Monsters

by Julie Doxsee

Black Ocean
Boston · New York · Chicago

Black Ocean
P.O. Box 52030
Boston, MA 02205
blackocean.org

ISBN 978-1-939568-03-8

Library of Congress Cataloging-in-Publication Data

Doxsee, Julie.
  [Poems. Selections]
  The next monsters / Julie Doxsee.
     pages ; cm.
  ISBN 978-1-939568-03-8 (alk. paper)
  I. Title.
  PS3604.O9545N49 2013
  811'.6--dc23
                                    2013005161

FIRST EDITION

Table of Contents

THE NEXT MONSTERS

CABIN

THE LAST MONSTERS

THE KEY TO MOVING CORRECTLY WITHOUT RUNNING INTO OBSTACLES

MANSION

IN THE SHADOW I AM NOTHING

ADDITIONAL NOTES
AND ACKNOWLEDGEMENTS

THE NEXT MONSTERS

everything that fingers touch / has to be retold
—Cole Swensen

LIGHTNING

I chomp at the black, bats everywhere. I drag you to a little room to show you 116 photos—six orange ones of big mushroom clouds. *You are lucky you made it* you say straight into my eyes. I flail my arms and make a gesture like *the water is always flipping*. So you bring out the urn.

I capsize the urn and cover myself in a soot suit, feel something ugly disappear, then scream when a handprint appears on the hip.

Sometimes I hope for new blood while trying to start my birthday. Any suit of yours I slip into is a nice birthday.

I emerge from the little room and climb aboard a tractor then get off the tractor to board a boat in the middle of a long bleak storm. That was days ago. It is nice here now. I've been missing you though you mailed a bag of money. I spend a handful when I'm sad. Days ago on the road the weather crushed down and crushed the tulips and muddied the soot. Now the weather is a big blue man and I am a muddy small woman. The first thing I see from the water is a day-glo rainbow. It is a little strange, deceitful, and I climb to shore with nowhere to go.

HOLY DOGS

I am left monsterless, red tying its underbelly to me when we split. I remember the skeleton's eyes looking blankly back as neighbors filled the temple with cut-off rabbit ears. Poking out from behind my statue of St. Mary for days, I remember the holy dogs in orange tissue encircled by torches, their silks snaking toward the monk.

I remember a hollow scream that hurt so hard as the holy dogs died. I left them gazing at their bleeding fronts and ran. The way Zeus splits a beast too powerful, they were split and we too. I couldn't walk alone near the street puppies later, near where the temple flushed its screams. So the universe peels back for days and we with it.

I remember many bowls of blueberries set at the foot of a stone alter. I was left monsterless, red rivers full of coins, the pillowed heads soft in orange tissue encircled by torches, the monks at midnight dressed in yellow leaves, a sort of hatching boring out of me. The sun set at midnight, one end of a hot cry retreating to its hiding place.

I stared up from a burnt picture of the way Zeus split my crown so hard until I was you. I am you. I stared up at the skeleton for days and couldn't walk for myself. There was a glistening twilight in the dew trees, a can of hot ash I hit my head against. The extra stripping away is a beast that wrenched out of me when we split.

I remember the monks dressed head to toe, the soft temple dogs running into their field like usual. I remember this hatching feeling, this clean pain, the whole ceiling widening and then the whole ceiling catching on fire. I remember wiping my knuckles over coins and shaking. I couldn't walk for days.

I am you. There is a hollow sound the universe peels back only for me, there is a stinging hotness only the loudspeakers chill. I remember when the holy dogs died. I remember the way Zeus split the goodbye fifty-fifty and flung its halves into the wind. My head was against the sunset at midnight, against a hollow sound only the red underbelly could hear. Three monks offered a dead bird with one shot-out eye.

I am left monsterless, I am a red river in surrender. I am you: my head gone, my head against. Beastliness was routine to me, the kind my heart was against all these years. I have sprouted from the universe, from a broken loudspeaker no one heard. The extra stripping away is a beast wrenching the lovers apart and wrenching the holy dogs from the temple. The dew trees spill water from me and from me.

GANGES SPIRIT

I am a hash mark full of pocket holes, taken from the journal of a hunchbacked man on his way to the noose. The ox is too big and the cardboard box nary hammered. In the bicycling wilderness, a fort depicts big waistbands the glory birds emerge from. And what would emerge is a horrifying template full of systems and formulas, beak-marks and lion tongues, gasping in the rain for the rain you loved. I can't understand the limits under-planking the shavings of water, ships burning on the strait while a lone man plays cowbell with a copper baton. Who went limping past to plea for a suicide near the yellow tree with a big blue eye painted on it? I want your tooth to bite a different kind of me until it compliments the blood. Do you understand how to turn yourself into an infinite reflection whose head always obscures the view? The messy histories of a bird running over puddles. The messy histories of a salt factory. Hounds, hounds, hounds on the suffering banks—what of them? We barge in so delicately in slippers made of down, made of holy petals, made of milk.

QUESTION
for Sampson Starkweather

Somewhere under seven layers of bone I promised an overdone disguise. You see my nametag and know the mangled piece of rain I store under my throat. Know the bright cheetah tooth I wield like a sunblind mountain on my palm, foreshortened in the dim window I reach to punch out of.

In one Istanbul back alley the shops sell only cheetah suits, the kind you would wake up the next morning in.

Another alley's shops sell only mannequins. Another alley's shops sell only handguns and ski masks. Another alley's shops sell only stuffed alligators.

I took two photos of 100 mannequins on a day the air was having at itself from the top down, cumulous by cumulous. There were no faces, only about-faces, the vulnerabilities of spine a row of right parentheses, naked and frozen, closing the question: what did we hope to embed in this kind of light, and would we have recognized openings without the shallow creases of closure? These very human creases?

As Rimbaud says, if you fall in love with a piece of avalanche, you must treat it like magic.

Another alley's shops sell only umbrellas and tinsel. Another alley's shops sell only disco balls with dog breath inside of them.

I wrote a long essay about your bird affiliation, an ode to what you are doing over there where when you count to five you say bird, bird, bird, bird, bird.

When you count the sky, you count the small shadows the realm's objects cast.

Every single bird has seen the flaring nest and all are perfect plus signs with heart shards for feathers.

I found a bird next to a mirror, a cardboard box, and a naked little boy who was frozen and unable to hear the whine of trees. I believe this was a version of you that came from a piece of my shoulder. You are the accidental sonic artifact of nobody's museum: the hand in the puppet's gut when every emergency screams pianissimo.

NOTE TO A SPIRIT SEER

What a man and woman say after hello could be *liquid glare*.
What a man and woman say after hello could be a fragile echo
funneled through the very first megaphone. A sort of jail cell
governs every word, conjugating immobility till deeply numb.
Kisses crack, coil, recite.

This is what I mean:

A man and woman who live in the middle of a town-flattening
tornado made of one million quiet sweaters may never know
devastation.

When a man moves from horizontal to vertical, the spirit of
his chair stirs and spills into the road, the beautiful filth roils
like a furriness peeking over cliffs.

WATER BAN

To be thirsty and to be scaled down to a beast with insect skin putting your mouth where the dry air meets your expectation with a dark spill of shadows. You search through the room with your hands, press them against the windows to make the water come out. This is your city. They yell through megaphones while the laundry rots, dishes rot. Your voice is a small cry stuck under the wing of a beetle.

You remind me about families who own little silos that fill with rain. When the weeklong water ban starts, children transport pails from the silo to the back door where their mothers cook rice in cloud flavors. Unlucky families discover monkeys bathing in their silos. Monkey-proofing goes only so far these days; the more we talk about opposable thumbs, the more the monkeys embody their power.

FROZE

The dimes on each eye grew, grayed. It was a *something that's mine and don't touch it* driving flashbulbs over the elephant of the evening, driving very much the black T-shirt through a small opening in the brick that very much made you smear me on the naked fog for a valet patroness.

Valet patron: You dropped your red scarf near the spice tray.

Valet patron: It is colder than sex igloos. It is colder than igloo bone. It is colder than fish spine.

A porcelain shelf shall calcify, shan't it, the glass mump on the jaw of jealous shells.

We have forgotten the elephant song; the song filled an elevator and died.

I see its vapors.

A frozen leg and a frozen arm clip a downed tree's electricity in the heavy *don't* of morning. The heavy *don't* is headless, hairless. I reach up to feel its head but there is the sharp blue edge of a bald neck—no head—then a space. The space comes down hard and clamps over my mouth until it pulls the shape of my lungs into its lungs, mine deflate and the frozen leg remains, but I see the frozen arm do its push up over me so suffocation becomes an animal with plastic eyes that when I talk it can. It can cockatoo talk. When I talk it turns electricity-city.

11

To count the floors the elevator carried, to do so shyly near a perfect thirteen-dollar pancake nestled in a bucket of ice, where the freezing enfolds all matter leftover from the moment when you notice there is no more to spill, there is a land-of-no-liquid the voices go underdone in, every bone a dead pin and needle so still.

BLUE KILL

I had a dream that he killed the sun by bloodletting the ram, by draining its heat. Sitting there to the left was the day. Staring at him were a sleeping woman and a knife.

My friend quit alcohol 16 years ago after drinking six liters of himself. He stared at himself. Two hours later his eyes made a flood. They broke most of the mirror, looked at a mountaintop and never woke up. He barely knew who said *I barely knew the man*. He killed the middle of the mirror after a sleeping woman who lay facedown on his right handed him the knife. He sat straight up and saw his own ghost. My friend spent most of the night bloodletting the bed. He looked into the ram's eye, drained its blood and looked to his right. He walked downstairs to another sleeping woman. The ram also looked into his eyes with big brown eyes. They spent most of the day staring at each other, then his wife called, hysterical, and screamed she had had a dream that he was dying.

My friend walked through the middle of vodka by himself until he found the knife, then looked into the mirror at a sweaty, blue-white, translucent version of the ram. Its blood flowed all over hotel room 201. After waking up in the day to stare at it, he answered the phone. Two hours later a man he barely knew said his wife had had a mountaintop-dream that he was dying. He stared. Two hours later his eyes flooded. A man he barely knew drove him to find help. The man was a sweaty, blue-white, translucent version of night.

GIRLS ON THE RUN /
TWO HOURS ON THE ISLAND

I am what I remember. I am a life whose heart was so close it tongued you when you were old enough to live within the two hours and old enough to see 25 kinds of what exists within the dunes. I remember the last fisherpeople left coconut milk to swarm with crabs; blue on the moonlit dunes, blue on the small island of huts. Around the crabs swarmed 13 children, boys, and those boys I remember made a landscape of handholds below where one airplane a week would fly over.

I remember the skin you were old enough to shock and lightning so rich the corncobs still in their husks popped. I remember the dunes. To celebrate in an ungoverned realm the bees must live in harmony with the snake-seekers someone said. A woman covered the girls' arms in bat blood so they wouldn't grow hair there. To envision a pink bike rolling past, you must slip a fish into the moonlight someone said. Where we lie now in two hours will swarm with 13 children, boys, and all will slip their imaginations toward the girls peeking from the green hill, bat-blood arms frailly flailing like bat wings. In an ungoverned land a slick and subtle shock brings lightning cut from the next monsters.

One uncle says the way to become a beautiful firefly is to celebrate the parrots, even, to offer their green feathers, beaks, acorn-sized hearts—and everything else they have—cut out, cut open, and itemized, to the beast family. Later in the shed he shucks off his jeans down to the skin as a present and there his penis hangs like a melted elephant nose.

To be on the run is to be a week overgrown with green, green hills; a gift of emeralds rolling from one end of the cradle to the other to mimic the flight pattern of an animal with no ears. Offer your green and subtle shock to the core before you throw the lightning into the pot. Only one airplane a week lands on this island, and it is a sick surge aliens feel when they discover skin made for men's pleasure sucks clouds out of the air.

The family, the core opening up before you from the beasts I remember faintly. The moonlight. What we could withstand was cut from the ceiling and those born into it were bound and cut and tagged and branded and their baby teeth saved for spells. An uncle cascades in with a carved whistle as a present and later shucks his jeans off in a violent rip.

We lie, and we lie, and we lie, and after two hours I have 25 kinds of sex with you right on this island. It is like this island is ruled by the base of the core and it is ours too. I remember to make the children safe. This I remember. I was a life whose heart was rich and later it tongued you through the ceiling.

M

I am an unsolvable puzzle because I repent the ethers of hormone. If he is real, he is to remain the one I love to feel the jagged pieces of until my attention and its feathers turn adventurous (but I love to cocoon myself in a black cloak, I love to skip stones over the delicate modes of skin and then dart to a far, far pinnacle).

My heart engages its own feathers and picks up its own feathers from the surface and I begin to point my binoculars toward whatever defies this factualness. I begin to strum the surface of whatever logic uses to skip stones over its broken part.

MONSTERLESS

My soul fell out and fell straight down the stairs, then he half-smiled and I found a baby scorpion in his eye. The encounter with my house is lovely today because I found, also, a smile under the chair in the sunroom and my bruises disappeared, after which I fainted because I was glad to be no longer pulverized like a saint. In fact his eyes watched me until I turned a higher temperature and vanished into the wall and onto the slightest glimmer.

The magic 8 ball gave an answer and I want you to reply that the encounter was not one of putting two and two together. If I were a smile I would get bitten into. It terrifies me that the world contains the sentence: *No one here has to see me.*

CABIN

CABIN

I notice a mist at the door. He removes the door to suck my breath from the idea of entrance.

I feel behind it: a baby sweater, three-dozen broken lighters, a box from the woman who has been trapped there a year.

He leans against my breath and shuts out the woman who has been inside as mist flies to the top shelf of the closet.

He removes the feeling of death. The doorbell rings.

I have the power to separate us from my wishes, to talk right into the ear of death. He takes the box from the stoop outside. He removes a small house from it and pokes a finger through the front door. I have the power to see who is in there, small and huddled, but she is obscured and tries to suck my lungs.

Time goes by wet; green vines dangle down. Time evaporates within the secret box.

I believe a firefly is in charge of death. The doorbell rings. I feel wet, green vines dangling down from my breath and have the feeling of having been on the top shelf for a year. He shuts the box in the distance and leaves. After he shuts the lid the doorbell does not ring again.

I am a firefly in the small cabin. I look out of the eave. I look out of the peephole to suck my breath from the door and to suck my wishes.

I am in the closet in the cabin. In it are: a jar with a baby sweater stuffed inside, three-dozen broken lighters, and the feeling of the door.

I am separated from her; we are both consumed with the house. She evaporates the door to see who is there, but a clear view of death remains. The doorbell does not ring again.

I am separated from my lungs. Time goes by. I notice a mist. I notice a firefly crawling over the eave.

CABIN

The next morning my body is off obeying its nature somewhere far away.

I open the door to the afternoon, finally outside.

I open the freed woman and she rests herself on the bicycle path naked. We are at the time of day when one half of the pond is black and one half of the pond is yellow and each third of me is moving slowly away from the other. I want to work.

I trip over the shadows of twigs on the ground.

She says hi and slips into a pantsuit and I pass through the atmosphere as though it were a shimmer.

A pregnant woman bicycles past. Sunup is off obeying its nature. I want to barricade the light with my body, but instead I follow her.

As I walk I try to light the lighters and fail and throw them against my foot until my foot is full of red marks. I pass the pond. The pregnant woman has gone into a cave, where I notice that perhaps the gray floor cools her. She rests her bicycle flat on the gray floor and closes her eyes.

She says hi and each third of me is pinkish and separating. I trip over the shadows of day air. Someone has painted the shadows of twigs onto the freed woman's legs. One half of day is gone.

I walk backwards out of the cave for a long time. Someone wisps past me.

She says hi and one third of me is a nothingness spilling into the ground. She says hi and two thirds of me are off obeying their natures somewhere far away. I trip over the thick mist.

The lighters are broken and I notice that perhaps because of the day air she wears red lipstick. She is gone in the thick mist. In my hand is a jar with a baby sweater stuffed inside.

CABIN

I am at the cabin. My husband has come back to barricade the front window.

I remove the window shade. He loosens his tie very carefully, as if he is swinging a heavy statue. My husband is drenched head to toe and is shaking. I want to say nothing at all but I ask if him if he is shaking. I move to the side shaded by trees. There is a metal gun cold in his hands. He looks outside and I look outside.

The woman has gold ribbons in her hair and her hair is wet. I am shaking. I see her sink all the way into the water on the black side of the pond.

Her face is frozen like a statue's. I throw a fistful of lighters at his hand. I see his hand drop the gun limply and his fingerprints move to the table.

I say again *are you shaking* but I begin to change, to very carefully help him get his tie off.

Again I test each one and my thumb cramps and I throw them into a corner of the room. *I didn't see you at the pond this morning* I say.

He squeegees his fingerprints across the wood. Metal grinding against metal is the sound of the lighters as I test them. *I didn't see you at the pond this morning* I say.

The lighters are broken, empty, all of them. She has gold ribbons in her hair and again he doesn't want to say he was there. I take his hand off the table and squeeze it. I ask if he wants to drown.

I make the sounds of plastic hitting wood. My husband at the window loosens his tie and points to the pond. *I tried to shoot her all day* he says. He points to the pond so that I realize it is not raining. He loosens his hand. He tells me he's been trying to drown all day.

I say *but I am helping you.*

My husband is holding a fistful of metal. I grind metal against metal all day with no fire. I was there to change the sounds of the water. He loosens his tie, drenched head to toe. I ask again if it is raining and I ask again are you shaking. I was there in the back of the box in the back of the cabin. I look at the yellow side of the pond. He says *I am shaking.*

He says he tried to shoot her all day and I ask again if he doesn't want to change the sounds of the water.

CABIN

He says *but you did see me, you saw me drowning.* At home I look and look. *I was firing bullets off underwater as though sending them back to the morning* he says.

My fingers gather around his neck frantically. *I was firing bullets as she stood over me and you saw me* he says. *You saw me and yelled at me to stay on the yellow side.*

We watch the surface where her golden ribbons sank. Colors seem meaningless now, like a form that has never occurred. *But you saw me* he says.

I throw some twigs into the box. I stop my fingers when he can't breathe. *I was submerged to the neck* he says *and now look. I can't see her* I say.

I want the lighters to cause an explosion.

CABIN

I imagine the pregnant woman lying in the cave next to her tipped bicycle, handlebar sticking up. It looks wrong, like a context contained in a form that has been stuffed into its last vapors.

Trees swallow the cave. Trees swallow the pregnant woman entirely.

I run back to the cave. The pond engulfs the evening as I run by. I kick the surface; I leave the water as a perfect thing. The horizon of trees swallows the cabin and I can't bear it.

Helplessness is down there somewhere. *But you don't see me now, you saw me before* he yells after me.

The pregnant woman is gone. I hang the baby sweater on the handlebars. It looks like a surrender flag, not a gift. The baby sweater is soft unstuffed.

I look and am submerged to my neck and frantically she stands over me saying something about how the water is a gift. I am on my way back to a form that has graduated into helplessness.

I feed a handful of twigs to the answer. The last vapors of butane are a horizon left for him to stuff into the box. They seem meaningless now. *But you saw me in the water, in the water in the morning* he yells. *You said you couldn't see me, but you did see me, you saw me on the water next to her!*

THE LAST MONSTERS

SUMMARY OF A MOON FILM

When the front door opens there are some broken off pieces of man there on the welcome mat. She is awful to accept such deliveries. She once loved the man and never touched him, they just played tug-o-war with a long piece of silk.

I watch her in an alley. She is so alien, like a prostitute. She picks up her own hellish, claustrophobic isolation and throws it. I watch an important messenger tell her something.

She is unaware of the little bits of fabric the man would sew into her palms: in private she squelches her poise and it is awful to hear silence exist in such a perfect American accent.

He carries silks and batiks on his way. She is in love with someone she can't open her pain in front of. She has spoken only once in her life, and it was a long time ago, and it was about a city full of rivers. In public her desire is so painfully fraught that it crumbles down. In private she can't open her mouth.

Between two hours lies the rest of the woman. This moment, at the end, of course, is when she tries to eat rice. She picks up a little picture of a city, elegantly spare. There is a world between the viewer and her mouth.

This moment will crumble down her chin.

The servant sews words into his tongue and stays in the same two alleys witnessing this painful exchange from a payphone. O her elegant robes, O her elegant robes.

Her master wafts by and no one speaks. They walk in and out of the same two rooms, holding the silk. At the end she can't perform her duties and carries a basket of rice to the city, speaking in English about the rivers there. There is a prostitute in the audience who can't locate her throat.

RED KILL

She wrapped herself in a shredded cape she found and threw a black stone into the blue water to cool it. When she lived with his hand in front of her eyes, the gray went after him; the gray abandoned her face and followed him. The girl from 1608 made her getaway, then she stopped and rusted his sweat onto a metal wall. She dug a big hole in the back of his house and filled it with coal. The girl from New Guinea molded his shape onto the right piece of blue. This cooled the metal wall.

His shape found the air under a piece of earth, and she lives with that loophole. The girl from 1608 started the good grace of cooling coals. But when she found an earth-covered piece of paper with his name on it she ran. *Red Kill.* No one should throw his shape into the pit.

Dear *Red Kill*, when you throw a girl from the side of the earth, do not look at her hand.

From his hand sweat poured like black lava. You live with the medusa from New Guinea. She handed over her eyes and sank into the hot.

BUS CRASH

I will shatter and stand behind myself, sniffing. Traffic was bigger than one fuck you. You are amazing. My power went off and on. Still when I tried to light a cigarette, a man walked up and threw a bag of fish guts on my foot. I went flying into the good as soon as I could. But then I was in a bus crash. Sound of awkward ticking stagnancy. Finally I have grown so many feelings.

I don't know why I see the happiest people ever when I walk into a downpour. Within moments the earth ticks and blood comes out. I am thinking my veneer doesn't match many veneers. First I shatter and then I land in front of the hot man. I yell nonsense at my foot. Then the bag of fish guts.

He put one of me on like a coat. I was in front of a giant fuck you and still behind myself, the second me deeply stagnant in the road. Traffic was in book form, closed, and I felt a minor whiplash. It was a rear end accident, which caused me to go flying. I flew after you this winter. I ventured out when I felt the city eat me. But after this winter what should I do? I got on the good bus and the man with the fishing pole dropped his bag. Glass smashed into my skin. Sound of receiving alternating messages. The happiest people ever softened it with rainwater. What else could I do? I was still behind myself, cold and accidental. I was still behind your skin.

LION TOUCH

Something important is nothing. To be inside people teaches us inwardness, doesn't it? A certain kind of me falls inside like an assumption. A certain kind of prayer finds a newborn you. Three days of water-only leaves a great pain in your chest without shoulds to cover it.

Something important is wow. Perhaps we are coloring the bravery it takes to make love, to stay anesthetized outside. I think so. I think most people live in our chests without a way to get out. To feel them there is zoo-ish.

I'm glad people stay alive. I'm glad I am naked.

PINK UMBRELLA

Today I'm mean because I ought to memorize joy.

I always feel a pink umbrella opening in my butt.

I always feel rainbow polka dots become very hostile when they single-handedly ruin the rain.

The alien in front of me totes one. I'm so silly, learning to be in charge of my feet. He single-handedly ruins the whole village's feet. The alien in the rain, the alien in charge of me bores a divot in the sidewalk. He single-handedly ruins my memory.

PINK UMBRELLA

Under sequined sarongs the earth revolves, but the joy of nearby villages blinks. For example, I was more depressed than usual after mouthing off, so I know. It's classic: he tries to disguise my authority but only on the weekends.

So over the weekend I blink at myself in the mirror for hours on end, become more depressed than usual. I always want to be a sort of creature, a creature with pink umbrella tonsils undulating after you.

No one really buys the boiling-point. A heat wave is welcome. People staring at me thought such an object would attract too much attention. People stare at me joyfully, which undermines my foreignness in the end.

I'm still living in the folds of the weekend and I want to mention the nearby villages revolving around your little cosmos, but my tonsils are lost.

It's classic: the alien in charge of my personality warps me.

PACKAGE

This happens one by one.

My mittens are buzzing always—the reason my finger settles on your cheek like a gravestone.

I received your package with chocolate, coffee, shoes, a very tousled piece of hair and a rare Uzbek textile.

I would trump any minor impurity or any complicated reason why I spent every ounce of my imagination on you.

Your obvious purity of heart would bundle all things and send them into the holy crowd.

PACKAGE

Your something-something finds my bridal gown off-putting.

But I like where we hung out on your wedding night when every dish was clanking.

My home is one whose spiritual antennae are always buzzing, hobo-style, like a recent exodus.

You strike me as one who is worth a zillion dollars. I imagine you in a museum. I see every tousled piece of hair.

I wept some amazing stories. I send a package of them into the holy crowd.

STILL

I can't give you a tortured speck of me but I can offer a big messy engine.

My hauntings are particularly active this week. For example, I am a white horse standing under the full moon. I wish I'd photographed it all: a black cow and a messy horse getting messy.

I hope everything is a white horse standing in the world getting messy.

I hope all is a speck on a hug or a hug on a speck.

For some reason the sky is your cosmos but I can't give you a reason to stand in the sky.

IN MY

I am in my head at the moment because of the fog of this man. I get up and have wine, see a horrible cab driver and the full moon. In my head is the image of the street and on it a bunch of people in love with identity. I am underwhelmed by everything that happened a long time ago. Last night I saw an awful public domestic dispute that I need to reinvent. I didn't see him hit her, but she had to protect all of the children.

I could fall in love with a foggy image, all alone and helpless.

It is good that you told me another man was treating a beautiful woman well and was having wine under a moon. It feels as though someone inserted a whale into my heart. In my stomach, also, is the other night. I can't shake the image, I can't shake the full moon. It is the permanent, not the fleeting, that hurts.

LAST

You come out of the ditch sunburned, wanting breakfast in continuous sunglasses. At 10:00am your facial scuff shone. Drudges make slants of the perfect light you let the low light counterfeit, champagne flat since the first pour. Pout about how air wanes. I wind up holding your long-lost suitcase in my fist after unbinding my hands. You pick me up fireman-style.

You have nobody to stoke the potent fuse. I climb to the roof alone. I never open it. The gutter rips open my side. You are stranded on the marble balcony somewhere above green rainbows and below traffic. Rain is permanent. Circuits bristle. I wait.

You arrive as though dropped from a southwest shanty in the year 2015, thistles in the beard you made thin. The impact of your pace in my gut. I forgot oxygen while loving its tendering of the blush.

I show you my side matter-of-factly as it bleeds on the tar. Stagnant clouds rush forth at every holy siren, then dissipate on the gravelly surface as water comes. This is how we leave the plant: more fragrant when bruised, more bruised when pressed by permanent thumbs.

You touch me with a watery hand. We stand on the roof cackling.

You hold the plant by its lower leaves and listen to the game as I sit with my shirt hiked up around my neck. Lightning. We thought of beaches full of hula dancers letting the show go on with muddy calves. This way. Slow looting of perception. The stain goes red. Dried urchin. That way. Many hands feel around in the air for full submersion, figure 8s and shells.

When you left I planted a dust bunny in the soil. A friend dared me to poke a knife into the hole in the latch.

✻✻✻

You became a dog. I became a frog. You became a lizard and passed me on the rock.

✻✻✻

The blood spins omens, 120 frames. You slip right past the velvet into me. We outlast the emergency siren, pouring glasses on the hard roof. The naked neighbor picks one book after another off the shelves. She laughs and shows her teeth. We laugh in the dark under a moon I can't see. It's the only thing I can't see, rubbed away by wind. A raccoon picks through garbage below. Later in the gutter she gives birth to a litter of babies and leaves them to wash away.

We expect more from the insides.

Kitchen packed, we chain-smoke in an empty house with red walls. The phone rings, there is a hexagonal shadow on the driveway and a small hexagonal sun. Days. The blue shell holding your years cracks easily with a flathead. I bend the latch back with my saliva teeth. I leave the socks dirty and flip through. Your spelling changes from page to page. Stain. A hunting knife to your heart. A photo of the fresh double cut and a song about when I tried to hide your scars in the back of my throat.

GIRAFFE TOOTH AND HELMET

You pull into a nook in the alley and my helmet clunks your helmet and this is a kind of talk we're having, but in the talk there is a kill wish and a rocket launch and a bright laser-beam lengthening our hearts across the sidewalk end to end. There is blood and light, and in the light a quiet. You pull a giraffe tooth from your pocket, center it in your palm and say *have you ever seen one of these?* From under my tongue I pull a giraffe tooth. I center it on my palm and say *yes*. We sit this way until the shadows disappear.

RIGHT NOW WHEN I LOOK AT ASIA AND COCOON

A flag unfurls like a sheet cracking over a bed over the sea. I love when sheets crack on their way from scrunched to flat over things. Ships, ships, ships bring things and people to people. A gull stares at a face and I stare at a face. The air is wet— nothing will stick to it except a deep lonely song. As a man boils cocoons he slips his naked hand in to pull the silk from private little worm homes, wombs. The song he sings is a scream for all songs lost above the torn submarines rotting black in the mud of the seafloor. Dolphins leap in the distance.

MOUNTAIN AND MONSTER

A hailstorm comes out of the monster's mouth and I spill my coffee with a jolt. We laugh and laugh as if we had come together for the only time and place when and where spilt coffee is funny. *You are the only monster I know who wears a pink sweater* I say to it as it pretends to offer me some cashews. We are on top of a jagged mountain, fingertips inches from the clouds.

ETERNAL FLAME AND LIP

The scene vibrant, the wood widened, twigs descend with feathery fingers to put us on the path. There is no moon, no talk; no wine so the dark is a long starvation. We reach the eternal flame with clouds of bugs. Rocks and ruins lie about invisibly. A small man roasts a sausage over the towering flame. It sizzles. *Can you think of the opposite of this?* I say with my blacked-out mouth. *Lost waterfall* you say, shapeless. The job of lips finished, we mix our hungers together, body and body end to end, and wait for something to crunch us.

MOUSTACHE

I was in love with a moustache. We ate fried mussels and hid under a winter coat in the monster cold. It made me wear big jewelry that caught the light nicely. It wanted me to coat my walls orange so I did. When it hovered in the streets, the streets became wavy and steep. The curtains turned to shiny leather and people, even, became wavy and steep. Groups of cats gathered near it one morning when it was asleep and took turns touching it with their paws. The moustache danced around on a face, above a mouth.

THE KEY TO MOVING CORRECTLY WITHOUT RUNNING INTO OBSTACLES

I have been sitting here like paper every day. Read me. Call me. Stick me in your ear and rear. I cannot reforest my landscape with horns. I cannot sleep windowless under a couch claw-shorn and beveled, nightmares budging at the liquid slick of the eyes. This is why I wear white eye-paint and the same blue dress and flip-flops.

I watch a man put white cocoons into a vat of steaming water. He reaches in to pull webs from the loosening cocoons. I, in the corner, wait for him to hand me a wad of cocoon string.

Against the wall other men dip their toes into buckets, and other men in suits huddle on a half moon bench while shrieking love songs. Each of them has a two-inch moustache and a lapel feather. They say *dance dance* in another language and a short skinny man with glasses stands up to flail like a baby seagull on hot coals. This is the east, and these are the lost songs whose singers are lost.

I choose this place for its wires and look what: I follow prisoners to a purple house where I discover someone has placed a large mug of beer in front of me—it is as big as a person. I say *I can put 8 triangles in my mouth* to the beer. I say:

I want to show you something. Come to the shed and look into this pail. What's inside it? You tell me. Tell me. I'm blind and have never even seen a pail or a shed or a show.

Silence is all I know. But when I reach inside I feel my breath turn hairy and my bones turn wool. It is rainbows, it is angel fumes, and I own them all.

I like words because they do anything right up front. I am a black cat with engorged nipples. My two babies are bats with goat legs. A third was born with white eyes—totally white—so it never saw my nipples and starved. For example.

When I look up I see a spiral staircase that goes nowhere and ends on the tip of a cloud, the lip of a rooftop—on a shingle, on a square where flowers continually burst from seeds no one can see.

Dead soldiers take a break to craft a birdhouse from pieces of tree.

One of them says *look, I bought a stone to hang around my neck—it is very old.* Another says *are there not-old stones?* And so the eyes go forward and blink

and both are very lucky to have eyes.

O meridian in the treetop, I am drunk. I am hula dancing in front of a picture of a pompadour. I have seen you looking through me and I'm gone. If you take ½ spirit and add bone and follicle, will this explain the hymn? One of the gods told me today that the key to moving correctly without running into obstacles is to place a pylon in the center of things and stare at it. I will never try this because it is not part of me. I will always be falling and will always be enjoying the plummet with a damsel expression on my face.

I have been married since I was 13—the year a goat kicked its hoof into my heart. Someone says I am always on the lookout for a goat to kick its hoof into my heart and someone is right. Words should find the physical and let it bruise, and they do bruise after one cuts them open to learn or to never learn how they tick. I don't want to watch your eyes crinkle and fill with oil. I want you to kick your goat hoof into my heart or step on my throat with your goat hoof. What protects us, really? The tunnel in the mind? A golden city in the clouds in the mind? Look for the teeth marks is the answer.

I remember when you touched me with your hands: 1000 yellow birds peeped inside my heart and lungs. And 1% of me died forever, 1% slid under a permanent umbrella and this is all a kind of blindness and an umbilical cord that strings from my heart to yours through obstacles and other sounds and air.

This is what I like about pain and living. It is always ending over and over forever, and it is always new. Cool air is a music and a chair to sit in. Will I find a solid rest? Only if people scream loudly enough that their voices become a hammock surrounded by constant drum beats and cocktails and other sounds and air.

It is time for valor and honesty: when I look under your wing and into the bottom of your glass, I see dust. I need to be thrown down and kissed and the air smooshed out of me. It is a basic need more important than food or sunglasses. Nothing else makes sense. Please do it or I will destroy the walls bit by bit with my fingers.

I am old. Do you see? I am an animal without a heart. I may be single-celled. In my dominion you touch my knee with a particular hand and I thrill. You worship. I thirst and scream and someone should cut off my hands so that I may live a normal life. I know I will die in a hot fire. If you sleep with a god, you will enjoy his firm tongue and lip-hold. I don't care for ugly people or barking dogs or spills of honey. From a different angle you look like a lamb standing in a puddle. From a different angle I stroke the air with my ice cube hand.

MANSION

MANSION

My whole body hums, and I tend to it everyday. When you see me wearing only voodoo dust we will need ice, of course, to quiet the smoke alarms. Meanwhile my gut hums and I pretend to keep a mountain under my pillow.

You see me aflutter in my expansive thorn garden, fresh from a 5-week coma, chanting *stillness stillness stillness issues velvet*. My hunger is unbearable, like a tight suit.

There are 22 rooms here your words inhabit—the twisted serifs I spiral up and corkscrew down and spiral up and corkscrew down everyday. Wear my dizzy skin, please, and shh.

What would happen if we became holy? My heart is a mansion with a thousand smoke alarms. What would happen if I didn't stop?

OCTOBER

The wild dogs are spooky so I give them candy. After delicious restaurants everything carnal dissolves until there is only you to do. Until then, others see you standing there like a quiet city in which the children eat ruined pumpkin, supervised, skin sending out immaculate halos. The wild dogs howl and I drink coffee until I go deaf. I hand these offerings off.

I found in my prison a dream, I found a dream that was extra ghoulish. There were howlings and I think about them every day with skin buzzing insanely. This week is as big as a city. I'm here and you will shatter 100 airplane windows before I emerge.

SORRY

How beautiful: there was a falling star. I was a falling star too, glad to crash into this roof. The other day when I was a lightning storm I hallucinated blue spaceships on my drive home.

I am sorry that I was a falling star and that I caught fire to the red curtains and the whole room. Sorry.

FLIGHTPLAN

Your flightplan is inside my voodoo jar and it smells amazing. I mean, your flightplan is on the tip of my tongue. Last night I put gold dust on your face right here and showed you the part of my arm where I wrote *an amnesiac said hi to me four times in a row each time seeing a new person.*

The breezes are here and in a few weeks they'll go amuck. I sat on the window ledge but it wasn't ready. I will open my voodoo jar and you'll know just what I dreamt about four times in a row, each time seeing a baby blink into the void.

Outside the window a suitcase bursts with soft bedding. When you are here holding the baby your smile will burst like soft bedding. I mean, I will give out blueprints describing the window and how to open it and I will leave the blueprints somewhere under my tongue for a few weeks and then you will arrive and find the details quite helpful and then she will appear in a convex sheen on your eye as you blink at her and she blinks at you and you blink at her and she blinks at you.

The breezes are here and I will save them for you. Until then I will open my voodoo jar and wish you could be distilled from this. I will draw one of the breezes on my arm.

IN THE SHADOW I AM NOTHING

ALBUM D'IMAGES DE LA VILLA HARRIS

The sun and horizon spit out a thousand daughters.

One is a sign coming out from beneath gravity in the shape of a book.

Or in the shape of parcels in the eyes that entomb every bird dispersing upward.

If one wants to return the baby colors to the body, one must deprive light of the statue it has become.

One day your blessed feet appear, appear, appear.

HOW BEAUTIFUL THE HORSES WILL BE
WHEN THEY TURN INTO REAL HORSES

In the eye of a saint one finds a blue jewel to store in the middle of the throat for up to one decade. In my dream was evil water; in my dream my hands pressed invisible windows into place.

I grew a second heart and buried it by the base of the volcano. Now it leeches into the soil of the whole world. My heart your bread. My heart your water, my heart your sandcastle.

The real horses have different muscles and live in one valley a monk carved out with a shovel. Can you imagine the eyes of this monk, his scraped body the funnel for a million tears? I saw a red confusion to my left. How beautiful the horses will be when they turn into real horses. Those eyes. Those planets we call eyes. In the extra thrum left somewhere behind the valley wall I am. In the small crack all a-sprout with clover I am. In your tooth I am. I grew another heart to spread to the dust, a counterfeit heart just to spread it.

THE EVIL WATER IN MY DREAMS

I thunder through you. I thunder my brain out. Do you know the equation of asthma, of objects I press? I press your heart between two panes, some of it leaks out the glass. Between my hands is a magnificent tango, a family of magnificent tangos we move toward as though they were stages of truth poking into our necks, staring into the light. Removing the birds from poetry and the animalism from helicopters are equally bitchish. Your ears satellite the wharf for clues, shadows. The night is only a twinkle and someday you will analyze where the twinkle fits on a scale of is to isn't. Any eye-piercing glare you must analyze burns into your airspace.

A CARCASS, A CARCASS, AND A DANCING CARCASS

What, when the body shrivels a memory, is left to chant unto the folding day—its bit of satellite left breathing—and *can you hear it, can you* and now what do we do, carcasses shivering? There is a code one may plug in to reboot the underbelly, to warm, to muffle it when it drops a tear or rips open from inside out. I can't stop *what would happen* and therefore the walls scratch me, every nail a new spot to open all alarm bells we drew from the place, the shape, the shape on my hip there like a frond, a spice, an ice handhold one uttered through the delicate teeth of his mother who sat on the floor wandering her mind to find a small fabric scarf she'd left floating in a puddle at the sight of 30 years of him spilling into the street palms-first.

I am smaller now and love to dance. Dancing is my cousin and in some countries our marriage is legal, expected. Maybe the possible shakes us and leaves us with a pair of twins we don't remember making love for, appearing for. And they cry our deep bones awake and they cry our deep bones out of hiding after they rise up from the tiles in scarlet cloaks. It is okay for them to soften us until the humors dance, until the humors spill the traffic of their infiniteness toward death, death, death; toward the rattles and bells, duets and pianos that make us a perfect thing.

When your carcass came it left a cave painting the color of sunset. I have built a small house around it and I have placed a teacup full of holy oil in the house's kitchen. The children line up to see it, the children run from the hills through these expansive gardens to see it. It is a painting of a small man feeding corn to a parrot in a cage. The parrot hangs upside down and we can't hear it speaking because sound is impossible to paint. The small man smiles and I want to know if he knows he is *here*.

IN THE SHADOW I AM NOTHING

Yet the handprint reddens, chokes. A small place on my leg embroidered, a rare moon summoned in the thick sticks. In the shadow I am nothing, a voice competing with stagnant microphones the city rooftops howl. To find a rooftop on the seafloor stings a heart. These cities underneath us pause in a dance, filtering hoof noise and rhythms of the proud shout. These cities above us: wasted volumes hushing a life woven straight from the shadow we move through like carcasses. What percentage of our lives is darkness? This is my affiliation: words are the scene of the last tree dying. Winter is the scene of the most insensible frond hanging on.

A beautiful eye opens, and also the sun. Something exits when form coddles the cookie-cutter twilight. Who brought you here? Who put you in my ear, a reverse image in the double-paned glass without anything to form? When one meets another back-to-back, not face-to-face, a click slips in to destroy the need for ears, mouth, eyes, nose, teeth, arms. Tethered to a chair, arms are the scaffolding of desire. What happens when our eyes are the accidents of encounter and the click undoes? *The earth widens* one might say, *and we fill the space newly opened around us.*

When a country enters the air, it is no longer inhabitable. We are always only a chamber of us, swirls collecting in the hourglass concavity, the external delicate point, the *almost nothing* fueling a sloth of minutes as they arrive at a point gravity assigns. Does this sound like truth? Does a 4000-page poem throw a mirror at the percentage of darkness we lose in a week of pink sunups? There is so much *no more* when we blink an argument toward its shocking brightness. When colors impregnate the body, the after-colors gain meaning. This is not the difference between day and night. It is the total space, the horizontal field we exist within face-to-face, an accident of logic we are not supposed to see.

VAPOR

A strange sadness forms a cult whose members are upper lip owners. A yawn falls off and forms a Stonehenge at the bottom of the glass. When you drink the roadblock remember to wave the other cars along and leave an extra hole to breathe through. Yawns were hoops to jump through extinguished, rough mane moving in space like seaweed, particular jaw partly stuck, partly sensitive against the camel fur. A vacuumed car hydroplanes the vacuum, and everything is *your skin is so nice* through the bit of yawn that was thank you.

Fourteen times and never again a spill of letters spells everything in order from first to last word; in birth order not alpha. Words rain. Words usher button-pressing ghosts from room to room and leave them there long enough for each door to open and close once. A vapor growls at us to spiral from the eyes to the lobby through the chest.

SOMEONE SLAMMED INTO A METEOR NAMED SOMEONE

According to logic there are puddles and the puddles are only puddles but what if. As you understand the higher place, what do you remember of the ungoverned manner by which science forks over its imps? And then the sun appears and it is the sun because it is the sun and not a puddle. How could it be a puddle. I am you and I have my sleeves and I have your arms and I have a swizzle stick in my chest. It happened when you asked me to stare into your eyes for a zillion hours and the meteors left heaven like a pack of hounds. Thus the stirring began. I will teach you how to drink a glass of smoke and you will know I know more than to sit aside while the rooftops fill with _____.

As you see, when I try to explain the substance a squeak comes out. An inhale explains better but means something beyond _beyond_ minus the means. A map of scars and divots explains better but I have no story to back them so they are forgotten. Still, in the paradise of sun, people leap the highest cliff to death. Does this fit the image? This is about gravity, actually, and about the long funeral we must have for it and for the first fall from the apple and the apple. There is no invention or origin. When we hunger we eat. When we hurt we analyze. It is language that makes an apple an apple and it is up to us to say _that is it._

So where does a windowsill fit in, or the skin of a sad elephant?

Nothing contains the noticing and how obsessed we are with it, peeking, peeking incessantly with empty faces. What will torque them, what will swizzle them to life if not a swallow of smoke sucked from the dried husk of a frond shucked from a hand that ran its knuckles over thin dew and plugged into us, into your mouth and my mouth, brought closer by another strange hand that reached out of nowhere with its coals and behind it a noise that sounded "orange"? The way I think of a place on your hip or lip saves me and saves me and when I feel like an empty hotel, still I am saved and saved and saved.

NOTES ON TITLES:

"Album D'Images de la Villa Harris" is after the book by Emanuelle Hocquard.

"The Evil Water in my Dreams," "How Beautiful the Horses Will Be When They Turn into Real Horses," "In the Shadow I am Nothing," "A Carcass, a Carcass, and a Dancing Carcass," "Someone Slammed into a Meteor Named Someone" are after the works of Jerome Rothenberg.

∗∗∗

ADDITIONAL NOTES:

"the accidental sonic artifact of nobody's museum" from "Question" is adapted from Sampson Starkweather's "A Limitations of Birds" (after Landis Everson) from *Typo 12*.

∗∗∗

Thanks to the editors of the following journals, in which pieces from this manuscript first appeared: *Phoebe, Denver Quarterly, Black Warrior Review, The Offending Adam, Sleepingfish, Kelsey Street Press feature, HTMLGIANT* and *Glitterpony*